Writers' ink
A Hewett Anthology

Introduction

Daniel Tilsley,
Outreach Lead on "Writers Ink" and Hewett Librarian.

Welcome to "Writers Ink", a creative writing collaboration between UEA Widening Participation and Outreach and the students of the Hewett Academy in Norwich. A group of students were invited to take part in an amazing opportunity to find their critical voices—the results of which you now hold.

The students were asked questions such as: Why do we review? What is the point of reviewing? Who reads reviews? What are judgements and how do we make them? How do we back up our judgements? The wonderful Hewett Academy students were given four-weeks to answer these questions and put together reviews of their own. These reviews, the hard work of these brilliant young writers who have a bright future ahead of them, are collected here in this little book—beautifully edited UEA's student ambassadors and published by Egg Box.

Some will tell us why The Dragon Price is great for LGBTQIA+ representation. One will explain why, if you want great character arcs, you go and watch Star Wars. Others will consider why Doctor Who works so well as a show—and why sometimes it does not.

Early in the project, because many of these students are avid Whovians, we sat together and watched an episode of Doctor Who, the famously terrifying Blink by Steven Moffatt from 2007—an episode that quite literally sent me flying behind the sofa back in 2007. Of course, the students were much braver than I was... because they approached the episode equipped with the tools of the sharp-eyed reviewer.

Diversity and inclusion lies at the core of all work done by UEA Outreach—and it sits at the very heart of "Writers Ink". "Writers Ink" aimed to empower our young authors and give them the opportunity to find the voice that many of them did not know they had. Keep your eyes open, because UEA presents to you the top film critics, important video game reviewers, and influential tastemakers of tomorrow.

Writers' Ink 2022: Film Reviews

Dr Sophie Scott-Brown,
Academic Project Lead

Writers' Ink is an annual in-school creative writing programme sponsored and managed by UEA's Outreach team. The Outreach team focuses on supporting local young people to gain the skills, knowledge, and confidence they need to make positive choices about their future education. As part of this, Writers' Ink introduces students to the range of subject matter that they may encounter in an Arts/Humanities degree, as well helping them to hone their technical abilities in creative and critical writing. The project culminates in a book professionally produced by UEA's student-led Publishing Project.

I am delighted to introduce Writers' Ink 2022: Film Reviews. The authors of these lively and imaginative pieces are clearly natural writers and critics with a flourishing future ahead of them.

Contents

What Do We Look For in a Review?   10

Why Does the Doctor Who Universe Work So Well?   13
Jessica Daymond

Doctor Who: I've Had Enough of Martha!   15
Jessica Daymond

Star Wars   16
Alex Haymes

Magic in the Valley of Encanto   17
Sophia Harrison

Gory and Bloody Brilliant Horror Films   18
Josh Kiczma

Doctor Who: "Blink"   19
George King-Clarke

Alex Kidd in Miracle World: One of the Best Master System Games 20
Morgan Lewis

Apex vs Fortnite 22
Dawid Radosz

The Dragon Prince: A Truly Fantastic Story 23
Dante Syder

Noah's Top 10 Films, TV Shows and Video Games 24
Noah Toastee-Hill

Ewan Toll's Reviews 26
Ewan Toll

Doctor Who: "Blink" 30
Charlie Webster

Appendix: Example Reviews 35

What Do We Look For in a Review?

The students participating in "Writers Ink" devised a list of what they look for in reviews. Here is what they came up with:

- Consistency
- Characters: main hero, main villain
- A plot/avatar
- Storyline
- Lighting—dark
- Screenplay
- Side-plots
- Audio: sound effects, speaking
- Character depth
- Entertainment
- Genres/themes (magic, romance, comedy)
- Character death (Primrose, Oliver)
- TV quality
- Philosophy
- Morals
- Music
- Injuries
- Makeup and costume
- Credits

- Actor/voice actors (David Tennant, Jim Carey, John Barron, Bob Saget)
- Director
- Special effects
- Set builders/props
- Story animators
- Publishers
- Scriptwriters
- Spellings
- Editing
- Authors (Darren Shan)
- Illustrations
- References
- Advertisements
- Representation
- Visual artists (Roberta Ingranata)

11

Why does the Doctor Who universe work so well?

Jessica Daymond Year 9

The Doctor Who universe consists of five different shows/spin offs. The first being the original Doctor Who seasons (as the fans call it 'classic Who'), which includes the 1st-8th doctors and even more companions. The second being the 'Sarah Jane Adventures' which revolves around one of the doctor's companions, Sarah, as she solves mysteries with her mechanical dog, a sentient computer and her son. The third show being the 'Doctor Who' most people watch today. This is the most relevant one of the five shows considering it's where most of the fandom is to this day. The fourth is Torchwood, which is arguably the best spin offs of the whole franchise. Torchwood revolves around former (and future) companion Jack Harkness as he and his 'friends' keep a rift in time and space from opening. The fifth is Class. Class is one of the worst things that ever existed: I started the first episode and immediately clicked off, that's how bad it is!

Now that we have established the main shows, we need to explain the story. In the Doctor Who universe, there are many amazing and wonderful creatures (for example: Weeping Angels, Daleks, Cybermen and more) which creates a big and character filled show. One of the main species is the timelord, which is the main character.

The reason why the Doctor is such a good character is because they are not special (excluding seasons 11-13). They are just a normal Time Lord that wants to help humanity. This shows a more relatable and well-rounded character, which helps us feel attached to them.

The reason I exclude seasons 11-13 is because they ruined this and made them 'special' and 'different'. This made a lot of the fandom upset and destroyed.

But, in the end, this is all my opinion, and my opinion is that in the Doctor Who universe there are no exact heroes or villains, and an equal layout between setting, character development and storyline. In conclusion, these two things are why the Doctor Who universe works so well.

Doctor Who: I've Had Enough of Martha!

Jessica Daymond Year 9

Martha Jones, the Doctor's companion in series 3 of Doctor Who, is pretty useless and is just a substitute for Rose, the Doctor's companion in Series 1 and 2. Her character pretty much runs off with the Doctor and cries about it (which is only entertaining once, when Rose did it at the end of Series 2).

Martha runs off with the Doctor, immediately falling in love with him. She is a medical student, but that hardly ever helps. She does make a comeback in the next season (the season when she actually has a character and personality).

Martha's character would have been good if we had her after Donna, the Doctor's companion in Series 4, not before, because she is not much of a change in character from Rose!

Star Wars and Character Arcs

AH Year 9

I really like the Star Wars movies, I have watched them all many times.

My favourite thing about Star Wars is the character arcs. These are very interesting and are a key reason why I think that the films are good.

A good example of a character arc in Star Wars is Darth Vader's reaction to Obi-Wan Kenobi's death in A New Hope. When Vader strikes Kenobi down with his lightsaber, Kenobi's body vanishes. Vader then prods at Kenobi's empty cape with his foot. We can see in this that Vader is scared—he did not know that Jedi could do this. This is good character development because, in the prequel films, we see that Anakin—who goes onto become Darth Vader—believed that he was the most powerful Jedi of all. Before Vader kills him, Obi-Wan says: "if you strike me down, I shall become more powerful than you can possibly imagine." It is a sign of Vader's arrogance that he kills him anyway, despite Obi-Wan's warning. Vader believes that no one can be more powerful than him—but when he sees Kenobi's body disappear, he is afraid because, despite being the most powerful Jedi, this is a trick that he has never seen before.

This is just one of the many brilliant character arcs that the Star Wars films have to offer. I'd recommend them to anyone who enjoys watching great characters and compelling personal journeys in their films.

Magic in the Valley of Encanto

Sophia Harrison Year 9

I think that Encanto is an amazing film for families to watch. It's suitable for young ages to older ages and has some beautiful animations. It is set in the lush green Cocora Valley in Columbia and has some Latin American aspects to it. The show is full of vibrant colours that stand out and add to the cultural theme; the magical fantasy aspect, and the moral of how family is more important than having powers. It shows a very good life lesson to young children.

The film is based on a family called the Madrigals. The protagonist is called Mirabel Madrigal. The Madrigals are an extraordinary family who live hidden in the mountains of Colombia in a charmed place called the Encanto. The Encanto has made something called 'cosita'. This is the family's magic as a whole. The magic of the Encanto has blessed every child in the family with a unique gift however, Mirabel, has no power and is pretty much shunned by her family, but soon she realises that she is the last hope for the family magic that keeps them all together. With the help of her Abuela, Tio Bruno, tia Pepa, mom Julietta, sisters Isabella and Luisa and her cousins Dolores, Camillo and Antonio, can she save the family from their doom?

I absolutely recommend this to everyone to watch. It is one of my favourite Disney films in a while and it has such an important lesson about the bonds of a family. It is important to stick together in a situation of terror.

Gory and Bloody Brilliant Horror Films

Josh Kiczma Year 11

I think that gory horror films are really good because they are violent, funny, and out of this world. Gory horror films include zombie movies and splatter movies. They include many scenes which are so outrageous that they become funny, as you are not meant to take them seriously. They can be viewed as both horror films and as comedy films. They can also be really weird and show things that you really do not expect.

I think that weird and funny horror films are good, but I also like "serious" horror films—especially "psychological" horror films. Serious horror films try to be scarier without much gore by raising challenging and concerning themes. They can also be really scary even though you don't see much at all; what is scary is the things that your mind creates. This is why they are called psychological horror films.

Horror is a great genre because it is so full of differences and can have many varieties. On the one hand you have films which are so funny because of their ridiculously gory scenes, while on the other you have films which are terrifying and really get under your skin even though they don't show anything.

But my favourite are the gory horror films because they are just so much fun. In my opinion, the best horror films should have gore, humour, and also be serious.

Doctor Who: "Blink"
George King-Clarke Year 8

A Roller Coaster Through Time
Like anyone watching Doctor Who, I am fascinated by time travel. In the episode "Blink", Kathy is whisked back in time to 1920 while exploring an abandoned house called Wester Drumlins and encounters the devious Weeping Angels. It's a roller coaster ride, so you need to pay attention to who does what and when.

Alex Kidd in Miracle World: One of the Best Master System Games

Morgan Lewis Year 9

Alex Kidd in Miracle World is a game for the SEGA Master System, in which the titular character, Alex Kidd, goes on an adventure to save his family.

Alex Kidd in Miracle World has a pretty elaborate story. Alex Kidd is a young boy who lives on the planet Aries. He was born into royalty, but he was separated from his parents at birth. For years Alex lived upon Mount Eternal, learning the art of Shellcore, which is a power that makes his fists grow and allows him to smash stone with his bare hands.

One day, Alex comes across a dying man. He tells Alex that Janken the Great is taking over Radaxian and that Prince Egle and his girlfriend, Princess Lora, have been kidnapped, and King Thor went missing. Alex also finds out that he is of royal birth. Before he kicks the bucket, the dying man gives Alex a map and medallion. The man dies, and Alex sets off on an adventure to save his family from Janken the Great.

Alex has to play Janken (rock, paper scissors) against Janken the Great and his three henchmen, and then fight them to save his family. He successfully saves his brother and his brother's girlfriend, but his father is still missing. In Alex's later adventures, he sets off to find his father.

Alex Kidd in Miracle World is a great game with awesome graphics for its time. It's got fast-paced gameplay with a good level of challenge. I think that the rock paper scissors mechanic is fun, but if you lose against your opponent, you lose a life and you have to do the whole level again.

However, you can get items that help you win, such as the Pendulum of Truth, which allows you to see what your opponent is thinking, the Sukopako motorcycle which allows you to go at high speeds on land, the Suisui boat which allows you to go at high speeds in the water, and the Peticopter which allows you to fly in the air. These items are very helpful when you are trying to get through the level.

It is great fun though. All in all, Alex Kidd in Miracle World is a great game and, if you're a retro collector, you should definitely pick this one up. It's an awesome game for its time. No wonder it got a remake!

Apex vs Fortnite

Dawid Radosz Year 8

Apex Legends should be better than Fortnite on top-rated games. I started on Season 4 and currently it's Season 12. Every single season has something different to it.

I used to play Fortnite. I spent over £300 on Fortnite but ever since Season 10 it got worse for the original players. The game started to get boring as many new, younger players joined up.

I play Apex Legends because it's a fast-paced and tactical game. I like it because you can't build cover like in Fortnite: you have to find cover behind something. Fortnite is based on building and hiding.

The Dragon Prince: A Truly Fantastic Story

Dante Syder Year 9

The Dragon Prince is a show on Netflix that I really like. It is well-paced, has a great story, and is very fantastical.

The story, which is set on the fantasy continent of Xadia, follows Prince Ezran, his half-brother Callum, and an elf called Rayla as they set out on a journey to return a dragon egg to the Dragon Queen.

I really enjoy The Dragon Prince because of its amazing fantasy story – where the protagonists try to settle the war between magic and non-magic creatures. The story is well structured and well-paced; events move quickly yet the series never feels rushed.

What is brilliant about The Dragon Prince is its LGBTQIA+ representation and diversity. It is important for people from different backgrounds to feel represented by media, and The Dragon Prince really delivers.

Noah's Top 10 Films, TV Shows and Video Games

Noah Toastee-Hill Year 8

Films
10. Jurassic Park 3
9. Jurassic Park: The Lost World
8. Jurassic Park
7. Jurassic World
6. Jurassic World: Fallen Kingdom
5. Jurassic World: Dominion

TV Shows
4. Prehistoric Park
3. Jurassic World: Camp Cretaceous

Video Games
2. Jurassic World: Evolution
1. Prehistoric Kingdom
0. Jurassic World: Evolution 2

What Noah thinks is good/bad about Jurassic World: Evolution 2

Noah Toastee-Hill Year 8

Good:
- The graphics are 100000/100000!!!
- Music is amazing!
- The dinosaur behaviours are well orchestrated
- The roars are well replicated!

Bad:
- The dinos move unnaturally
- There are a few minor bugs

Ewan Toll's Reviews

Ewan Toll Year 8

I thought "Blink" was a great episode. The lighting was great, and the idea of the angels was timeless.

Also, Sally Sparrow (played by Carey Mulligan) was a great character! So was Larry (played by Finley Robertson). And the plot was top quality.

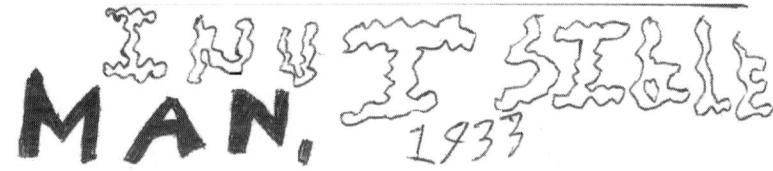

The Invisible Man is a classic horror film from 1933 that follows Dr Griffin who develops a serum to make himself invisible. He then goes on a killing spree. I thought the film followed the story of the book by H.G. Wells quite well. The special effects are fantastic.

Harry Potter and the Philosopher's Stone

I found Harry Potter and the Philosopher's Stone very exciting, especially the tune which was made by John Williams.

New Horrible Histories

As we all know, Horrible Histories is both educational and humorous. But in the new 2021 Christmas special, I spotted a new voice actor completely different from the original cast. I am also requesting they bring back Stupid Deaths.

The Lion King *(2019)*

I'm afraid to say that this version of Simba made me feel very disappointed and was not nearly as good as the 1994 cartoon, so it did not reach my satisfaction. Also, the story of the meercat and the warthog was much less interesting.

Spiderman: Far From Home

Spiderman: Far From Home and Spiderman: No Way Home are some of the best Marvel films ever, with humour around every corner, and terrific music.

Ewan's Favourite Films & TV Shows
1. 70's Doctor Who
2. Creature from the Black Lagoon
3. It Came from Outer Space
4. The Hitchhiker's Guide to the Galaxy
5. Indiana Jones and the Raiders of the Lost Ark
6. 60's Star Trek
7. Star Trek: The Next Generation
8. Star Wars
9. 80's Sherlock
10. The Book of Boba Fett

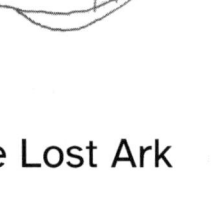

Favourite Books: The Harry Potter series
Favourite Video Game: Spaceflight Simulator

Good and Cool Films	**Bad and Budgety**
Maybe Dune	The Quartermass Experiment
It Came from Beneath the Sea	The Good, the Bad and the Ugly
Ghostbusters	
Ghostbusters: Afterlife	
Poirot	
The Trouble with Harry	
O Brother, Where Art Thou?	

Doctor Who: "Blink"
Charlie Webster Year 9

This episode of Doctor Who starts off with Sally Sparrow sneaking into an abandoned house called Wester Drumlins. While there, she removes the wallpaper and finds writing that addresses her by her name. The writing instructs her to duck and, "BEWARE THE WEEPING ANGEL!"

The episode follows Sally Sparrow and her life spiralling out of control. As the situation gets more complicated, she goes to the police. While there, the detective shows her a police phone box that was found, abandoned, at Wester Drumlins. This police phone box is the iconic TARDIS from the show.

I like the brilliance of this episode because of the Sherlock style investigation and the DVD idea, where the Doctor uses hidden DVD Easter Eggs to talk to Sally. This created opportunity for some amazing quotes such as: "THE ANGELS HAVE THE PHONE BOX!" The use of the DVDs means that Sally only finds out information slowly, when she needs it, which makes the episode more engaging.

I liked that an explanation was given about how the Weeping Angels work, and also about how the Doctor was able to communicate with Sally through the DVDs. The ending ties up this loose end which creates a satisfying conclusion.

I wish that we got to see more of the Doctor in the episode.

That being said, I think they handled an episode with little input from the Doctor well.

I also like the TARDIS scenes because it just shows how little of the TARDIS's abilities we actually know, giving a slight hint of curiosity

Overall, the Weeping Angels are terrifying creatures that have the perfect defence mechanism – they are quantum locked until you look away, which is when they get you. I also love the fact that they send you back in time, feeding off of all you should have been, while you are living out your days in the past and yet, in the present, already dead.

I like that in the police station they have multiple cars belonging to past victims of the Angels. I love the suspense and curiosity it brings that not only is the Doctor not there to help but that he doesn't know much about the Angels.

The only problem I have is, in the Eleventh Doctor's run, there's a plot hole around the idea that "an image of an Angel is an Angel itself". There's a scene where Amy gets an Angel in her memory from looking an Angel in its entirety, but Sally and Kathy do the exact same thing with no repercussions.

I also love the fact that, later on in the series, the Thirteenth Doctor gets put in an Angel form prison which may mean that the

Angels are a division unit of prisoners forced to carry out divisions' work. This also supports the theory of Weeping Angels being time lords. That being said, the Angels in that episode sometimes break the rules and move when people watch. The episode also shows that Angels can possess people

The lack of the Tenth Doctor in the original Weeping Angel story, Blink, is both brilliant and terrifying due to the fact that the doctor is always there to save the day. A quote from the Twelfth Doctor about his role says he is: "the man who stops the monsters".

Blink truly is Steven Moffatt's masterpiece and he will probably will be remembered as the man who created the monstrous Weeping Angels, which are a very recurring character in New Who. The creatures are intriguing as no one knows what they truly are, where they originate or how long they live, giving speculation that the Angels are immortal. This only adds to the spine-chilling creatures.

The fact that the doctor knows nothing of the Angels is why when the doctor fights the Daleks, Sontarans and Cybermen, the Doctor is angry or confident; but when fighting the Angels, they are terrified.

Appendix: Example Reviews

Negative review about OOglies:
Madeline Donnelly

The stop-motion animated television show OOglies on CBBC fails to excite as it contains little variety, and therefore quickly becomes repetitive. Whilst the idea of food products debarking on household adventures at first glance seems rather funny and sweet, there are only so many times you can watch different kinds of food—and on occasion, a rogue glove or a rubbish bin, all with stuck-on plastic eyes—gallivanting around different rooms, without losing interest.

Though the animation itself is executed well, this one strong point is simply not enough to make OOglies sufficiently entertaining. The current format of multiple short sketches, especially after so many episodes, fails to capture and hold the attention of the watcher for a significant period of time, a possible reason as to why the longer twenty-minute episodes have now been mixed in with shorter, 'fun-size' episodes. The show's lack of dialogue merely adds to this feeling of monotony. OOglies is tedious because it pedals out the same jokes time and time again and expects its audience to laugh as hard as they did the first time.

Every episode feels, if not identical, then certainly tiringly similar. In truth, each episode of OOglies that appears on our television screens seems to be a rather dull stepping-stone between more interesting television programmes. If I had to emphasise one good point of this show to justify its continued presence on television, I would say that it does provide an excellent opportunity to nip out of the room for a toilet break before something more exciting comes on.

The Big Review of The Lion King
(2019 remake)

Georgia Harris

After much anticipation, the 2019 remake of The Lion King was released in cinemas. As a devoted fan of the original 1994 edition, I was very disappointed by the result.

Firstly, the visual effects. The biggest advertisement for the remake was the use of live-action visual effects. Admittedly, the visual effects give a stunning portrayal of both the animals and the African landscape. However, since the live-action style is more realistic, the fight scenes are more vicious. This limits the film's appeal because it is then too scary for younger children to watch.

Secondly, the revision of the songs proved completely unnecessary, and in most cases produced versions that were lesser than the original. In particular, the new version of "Be Prepared" is more militaristic, as Scar recruits his army of hyenas. However, this detracts from the musicality, which was what made the villain's song of the original so popular.

Thirdly, the 2019 remake very obviously takes lead from the 1994 original. Iconic scenes are mostly depicted shot for shot, line for line, with only minor tweaks being made. Such close copying fails to honour its predecessor, and instead limits this edition's originality and highlights the insufficiency of the remake.

In conclusion, the 2019 remake of The Lion King was an unnecessary revision to a Disney classic. Overall, the visual effects and revised songs fail to improve the storyline, and instead make a film that is less family-friendly and limits its universal appeal.

Review of Adventure Time:
Leo Schrey-Yeats

Adventure Time is a profound show because it delivers meaningful storylines, wrapped in a highly imaginative and distinctive art style that is easy to adore.

Each episode follows the adventures and everyday lives of the residents of the colourful Land of Ooo, a world of infinite possibilities and potential. On the surface, many of these stories may seem purely innocent and whimsical—however, Adventure Time offers rich and complex plots and character arcs that are not afraid of delving into thoughtful—and at times even heavy—concepts and subjects.

For example, Finn the Human constantly grapples with questions surrounding his relationships, purpose and identity throughout the show. Jake the Dog struggles to come to terms with change and age. Starting as a comic villain, the Ice King becomes a tragic figure, as we begin to uncover his past as Simon the archaeologist and his madness-induced dissent into the Ice King. Even the deceptively innocent Princess Bubblegum conceals a dark agenda as she pursues her morally questionable personal ambitions with her science projects and a concerning desire for control. As a result, each character has an incredible amount of depth that encourages viewers to reconsider their perceptions.

In conclusion, Adventure Time is an undoubtedly innovative, profound and influential viewing experience because of the underlying depth beneath the imaginative delight on its surface, therefore allowing both young and mature audiences to enjoy it.

Encanto

Zoe Shakes

Encanto is the latest movie to be released on *Disney+*. It is a phenomenal and truly original film, which centres on a family with magical powers. Although the idea of magic might sound like standard Disney material, the way this theme is handled manages to strike on new ideas, presenting them in a unique way.

Encanto presents a nuanced take on the idea of a magical gift. While the movie effectively captures the beauty and wonder of magic, it also shows the negative side. All of the magical characters have unique powers—for example super strength, shapeshifting and the ability to control the weather. Along with all the benefits of such powers, however, come numerous downsides: the character with super strength has to take care of many tasks and is given too much responsibility; the shapeshifter isn't comfortable in his own skin. They all find their self-worth in their gifts.

Throughout the movie, though, they learn the importance of loving themselves simply for who they are rather than for their magical abilities. The movie teaches its audiences a positive message about self-esteem and what makes us valuable. It presents the moral of the story in a way that will be accessible and easily understood by a young audience—through songs and clear visual imagery—making it ideal for a Disney movie. The music, jokes and bright colours will all be appealing to children as well as adults, so will attract a wide audience.

Overall, Encanto is a fantastic and ground-breaking movie that I hope will launch a new era of Disney films.

ACKNOWLEDGEMENTS:

Many thanks to the UEA student ambassadors who helped out with "Writers Ink"; Madeline Donnelly, Georgia Harris, Leo Schrey-Yeats, Zoe Shakes and Max Wrigley, and to Dr Sophie Scott-Brown, Hannah Tough, Lucy Schofield, and Amy Mackrill, who got and kept the whole thing rolling (among many other things). Thanks to our publishers, Egg Box.

A very special thanks to Chris Hale who supported the project in Hewett. Many, many thanks also to Amy Lee and Rebecca Hill, the brilliant Creative team at Hewett who provided the space, resources, and encouragement. Last but never least, a gigantic thanks to Louise Rawlings, Elaine Furness, Sandyha Jayaraman, Annette Sinden, Alex Wynn, and Claire Rider, the Specialist Resource Base (SRB) team at the Hewett Academy who ensured the inclusivity and diversity of "Writers Ink".

WRITER'S INK

First published by Egg Box Publishing in 2022
Part of UEA Publishing Project Ltd
International ©2022 retained by individual authors
A CIO record of this book is available from the British Library

This book is sold subject to the condition that
it shall not, by way of trade or otherwise, be lent, resold, hired out, stored in a retrieval system,
or otherwise circulated without the publisher's prior consent in any form of binding or cover other than that in which it is published and without a similar condition including the condition being imposed on the subsequent purchaser.

Writer's Ink is typeset in Atkinson Hyperlegible
Cover design and type setting by Anna Brewster
Printed and bound in the UK by Imprint Digital
Distributed by NBN International

ISBN: 978-1-913861-84-1

Eggbox Instagram: *@theeggbox*